Quick Guide to Increasing Sales for Your Magnetic E-Book

Warren Brown

Published by Warren Brown, 2023.

QUICK GUIDE TO INCREASING SALES FOR YOUR MAGNETIC E-BOOK

First edition. February 11, 2023.

Copyright © 2023 Warren Brown.

ISBN: 979-8215166345

Written by Warren Brown.

Also by Warren Brown

Prolific Writing for Everyone
On Writing Magic
The Writer's Creativity Cave
The Writer's Oasis
Castle of Ideas and Inspiration for Writers
Chasm of Creativity and Inspiration For Writers

Standalone
Supernova: A Collection of Science Fiction Short Stories
Instant Poetry App
Mask of Evil: Adventures of the Storyteller
Vintage Tales: Eurasian Short Stories
Impostor Assassin
Camelot Crypto 1- Crypto Genesis
Camelot Crypto 2- Crypto Odyssey
Camelot Crypto 3- Crypto Symbiosis
Camelot Crypto: Three Short Crypto-currency Stories
Three Christmas Coins: A Poem
The Christmas Dimension
Happy New Year
Festive Delights
Coulrophobia: Empire of the Clown King

Creative Vibes
Rewrite Your Story To Become The Hero
Pandemic Blasters
New Year Odyssey
Pandemic Blasters Omnibus
Travel Man
Monkey in Mind
Masquerade
The Marauders and Mavericks
Mystic Inspiration Prompts for Writers
Cafe of Creativity and Inspiration For Writers
Quick Guide to Increasing Sales for Your Magnetic E-Book

Watch for more at https://warren4.wixsite.com/warren.

Table of Contents

Quick Guide

to Increasing Sales

For Your

Magnetic E-Book

By

Warren Brown

LONDON. UNITED KINGDOM, 2023

Chapter I: Introduction

Self-publishing an eBook can be a rewarding and fulfilling experience, but getting your book into the hands of readers can be a challenge. However, distributing your self-published eBook for free can be an effective way to reach a wider audience, build your brand as an author, and ultimately increase sales. By giving away your book for free, you can attract new readers, engage with your existing audience, and generate buzz for your book. If you have not written your eBook you should think about writing one today. With the power of an eBook you can attract a lot of interested new customers to visit your website, as well as become a recognized authority on the subject you write about.

Personal Reflections on Independent Authorship and Publishing

The Reasons I am happy to be an Independent Author in the 21st century

The First Story Which Made an Impact on My Creativity

The first story I read which made an impact on me was "Treasure Island" by Robert Louis Stevenson. The story was filled with action, adventure, and suspense. I always look for adventure and excitement in the books I read. This has in turn made me want to keep my readers gripped from the beginning of my stories as well.

The Writer's Journey

I first started writing poems, research articles and blogging, when I was a teenager. It is now 33 years since I have been writing and publishing on the web.

The Art of the Book Cover

The cover needs to reflect the essence of the story in my opinion. The cover design is an art, which I am still learning about. The cover should be able to generate interest in the mind of the reader. The cover is the first visual hook that the readers see even before the title. The title comes next in the reader's view and mind.

The Importance of Social Book Marketing

I use my blogs and my author's website to do my book marketing, as well as the usual social bookmark sites on the web. I even have an e-newsletter to keep my readers updated on my writings. Twitter is now my favorite social site for spreading the word about my writings. I find Twitter very useful as there are so many authors who offer other authors support and encouragement with their writings.

The Story behind "Travelman"

My novel "Travel Man"[1] is based on the freedom of the imagination which we all have, but which remains hidden. In the case of the character in the book, his mind and his vivid imagination play an important role in his survival.

Human imagination does have a very active role to play in our lives, and it possesses the power to change our lives and the history of mankind.

An Indie Author on Amazon Kindle Publishing

I enjoy the freedom of indie publishing. I am able to have full control over almost every aspect of getting my work published and ready for my readers to enjoy. I like the speed and the extensive outreach of writing and indie publishing. I have so many ideas for the future and I feel that indie publishing gives me the freedom I need to express my creativity.

I publish my short stories, novellas, and novel on Amazon Kindle publishing and on other platforms as well, such as Draft2Digital and Smashwords. I give my books free to readers, which has helped me to grow my reader base. I promote my books on Twitter and other social sites.

The Greatest Joy of Writing and Publishing

My greatest joy in writing and publishing is that I have the opportunity to give life to my ideas and to express my creativity. Completing and publishing a book is an exhilarating experience for me, every time.

Treasure Your Readers

---

1. https://books2read.com/b/travel4love

Every artist needs someone to appreciate his or her work. My fans are most important to me and I owe it to them to keep on writing and publishing more exciting and thrilling books for them. Thank you fans present and future for liking my work.

The Storyteller Series

The Storyteller is an adventure fantasy series about a man who discovers that he possesses the powers of Story, with the ability to craft and weave stories to fight crime. I was inspired by my father to create the Storyteller series as he would visit the Schools in the city of Calcutta telling stories to children, as well as on the radio every weekend.

Writing Influence

My Dad is a writer. He had a great influence on my writings. I grew up in Calcutta, India, and being of British-Indian (mixed-race) origin, it has also had a major influence on my writings.

On Becoming an Author and an Entrepreneur

Every author needs to become an entrepreneur. I have always been interested in advertising and marketing. This has got me involved in blogging and promoting my books on social media. My strategy is that I first write and publish my books, after which I spend one-week doing social media promotions on sites like Facebook, Twitter, Instagram, and Pinterest.

I have also joined a number of author sites on which I promote my published books. I enjoy writing, publishing, and marketing. I wish that I could publish one or two books a month. With the help of Amazon Kindle publishing and others, I can now publish more than one short story a month, which is just fantastic for any author.

Impostor Assassin- The Novel that is Closest to My Heart

My novel, "Impostor Assassin"[2] is a thriller set in a world where writing and publishing is the main source of employment. The novel focuses on one man's mission to create a market for Authors and Independent publishers. "Impostor Assassin[3]" is primarily about the future of independent publishing, with the aid of new and improved A.I. technology. I was inspired to write this novel by my dad's work in journalism.

Independent Publishing of the Future[4]

---

2. https://books2read.com/impostor

3. https://books2read.com/impostor

4. _https://warrenauthor.medium.com/the-renaissance-of-independent-publishing-impostor-assassin-9508a86a544e_

Why Distributing Your Self-Published eBook for Free is Important

Reach a wider audience: Distributing your eBook for free can help you reach a wider audience, especially if your book is in a niche market. By offering your book for free, you can attract new readers who may not have otherwise discovered your book.

Build your brand as an author: Distributing your eBook for free can help you establish yourself as an authority in your niche, and can also help you build your brand as an author. When people enjoy your book, they are more likely to look for other books you have written, and to share your book with their friends and followers.

Generate buzz for your book: Giving away your book for free can generate buzz for your book and increase the visibility of your book. By attracting new readers and building your audience, you can create a following for your book and generate interest in your other books or products.

Gather valuable feedback: Distributing your eBook for free can also help you gather valuable feedback from your readers. This feedback can help you improve your writing, refine your marketing strategy, and better understand your target audience.

In conclusion, distributing your self-published eBook for free can be a powerful tool for reaching a wider audience, building your brand as an author, and increasing sales. By giving away your book for free, you can attract new readers, engage with your existing audience, and generate buzz for your book.

Chapter II: Choosing the Right Platforms

There are many platforms available for distributing your self-published eBook for free, and choosing the right platform for your book can be a challenge. In this chapter, we'll discuss some of the most popular eBook distribution platforms and what you need to consider when choosing the right platform for your book.

An overview of popular eBook distribution platforms

How to choose the right platform for your book

Features to look for in an eBook distribution platform

An Overview of Popular eBook Distribution Platforms

Amazon Kindle Direct Publishing: Amazon Kindle Direct Publishing (KDP) is one of the most popular eBook distribution platforms and is a great choice for authors looking to reach a wide audience. With KDP, you can distribute your eBook in multiple formats, including Kindle, EPUB, and PDF, and make it available for free or for sale.

Smashwords: Smashwords is a digital publishing platform that allows you to distribute your eBook in multiple formats, including EPUB, PDF, and mobi. Smashwords offers a variety of distribution options, including free and paid distribution, and makes it easy to reach a wide audience.

Barnes & Noble Press: Barnes & Noble Press is the self-publishing platform for Barnes & Noble, one of the largest booksellers in the US. With Barnes & Noble Press, you can distribute your eBook for free or for sale, and reach a large audience of book lovers.

Kobo Writing Life: Kobo Writing Life is the self-publishing platform for Kobo, a Canadian eBook retailer. With Kobo Writing Life, you can distribute your eBook in multiple formats, including EPUB and PDF, and reach a large audience of eBook readers.

How to Choose the Right Platform for Your Book

Consider your target audience: When choosing a platform, consider your target audience and where they are likely to find and download your eBook. If your target audience is primarily Kindle users, Amazon Kindle Direct Publishing may be the right choice for you. If your target audience is more likely to use other eBook readers, consider Smashwords or Kobo Writing Life.

Look at distribution options: Consider the distribution options offered by each platform, including free and paid distribution, and make sure the platform you choose offers the options that are right for your book.

Check for compatibility with your eBook format: Make sure the platform you choose is compatible with the format of your eBook. For example, if your eBook is in EPUB format, make sure the platform you choose supports EPUB.

Evaluate fees and royalties: Consider the fees and royalties charged by each platform, and make sure you are comfortable with the terms offered.

Features to Look for in an eBook Distribution Platform

Wide distribution: Look for a platform that allows you to distribute your eBook to a wide audience, including multiple eBook retailers and libraries.

Easy uploading and formatting: Choose a platform that makes it easy to upload and format your eBook, and that provides support and resources to help you along the way.

Analytics and tracking: Look for a platform that provides robust analytics and tracking, so you can monitor your book's performance and make data-driven decisions.

Customizable options: Choose a platform that allows you to customize your book's listing and description, and that provides tools and resources to help you promote your book.

In conclusion, choosing the right platform for your self-published eBook is essential to reaching a wide audience, building your brand as an author, and increasing sales. Consider your target audience, distribution options, compatibility with your eBook format, fees and royalties, and features such as wide distribution, easy uploading and formatting, analytics and tracking, and customizable options when choosing the right platform.

Chapter III: Building Your Author Platform

An author platform refers to your visibility, credibility, and influence as a writer in the marketplace. It is essential for self-published authors to have a strong author platform in order to reach a wider audience, promote their books, and increase sales. In this chapter, we will explore the importance of having a strong author platform and the steps you can take to build one.

Importance of having a strong author platform:

1. Increases visibility: A strong author platform helps you reach a wider audience by increasing your visibility in the marketplace.
2. Builds credibility: By establishing yourself as a knowledgeable and authoritative voice in your niche, you build credibility with your audience and potential readers.
3. Increases influence: A strong author platform can help you influence others and promote your book to a wider audience.

Steps to build your author platform:

1. Define your brand: Identify what makes you unique as an author and the type of content you want to create. This will help you define your brand and establish yourself as a credible voice in your niche.
2. Create a website: Create a professional website that showcases your work and provides information about you and your book.

1. Utilize social media: Use social media platforms to reach a wider audience and connect with potential readers. Regularly post updates and engage with your followers.
2. Build an email list: Collect email addresses from your followers and potential readers and use it to stay in touch with them and promote your book.
3. Create valuable content: Create valuable content such as blog posts, videos, and podcasts that provide information and insights related to your book and niche.
4. Network with other authors: Connect with other authors and professionals in your niche and participate in online communities and events.

How to use your author platform to promote your book:

1. Share updates: Share updates about your book and other projects on your website and social media platforms.
2. Offer exclusive content: Offer exclusive content such as sneak peeks and behind-the-scenes information to your email subscribers and followers.
3. Collaborate with others: Collaborate with other authors and influencers in your niche and participate in joint promotions and events.
4. Host events: Host book signings, webinars, and other events to connect with your audience and promote your book.

In conclusion, having a strong author platform is essential for self-published authors to reach a wider audience, build credibility, and increase sales. By following the steps outlined in this chapter, you can build a strong author platform and effectively promote your book.

Chapter IV. Utilizing social media

How to use social media to promote your book

Best practices for promoting your eBook on social media

Strategies for engaging with your audience on social media

Social media can be a powerful tool for promoting your self-published eBook and reaching a wider audience. In this chapter, we'll discuss the best ways to use social media to promote your book, the best practices for promoting your eBook on social media, and strategies for engaging with your audience on social media.

How to Use social media to Promote Your Book

Identify your target audience: Before you start promoting your book on social media, it's important to identify your target audience and the social media platforms they are most likely to use. This will help you tailor your message and reach the right people.

Create a social media presence: Set up accounts on the social media platforms where your target audience is active, and use these accounts to promote your book. Make sure your accounts are professional and represent your brand as an author.

Share updates and information about your book: Regularly share updates and information about your book on social media, including new releases, promotions, and special events.

Share engaging content: In addition to promoting your book, share engaging content related to your book's theme or genre, such as articles, images, and videos. This will help build your audience and keep them engaged with your brand.

Best Practices for Promoting Your eBook on social media

Be consistent: To be effective, you need to be consistent in your social media promotion. This means posting regularly and following a consistent schedule.

Be professional: Always present yourself professionally on social media, and make sure your content is high-quality and engaging.

Engage with your audience: Respond to comments and messages from your followers, and actively engage with your audience by asking questions, sharing feedback, and starting discussions.

Offer promotions and incentives: Offer promotions and incentives to your followers to encourage them to download and read your book, such as exclusive content or discounts on future books

Strategies for Engaging with Your Audience on social media

Ask questions: Encourage your followers to share their thoughts and opinions by asking questions related to your book or the themes it explores.

Share behind-the-scenes content: Share behind-the-scenes content related to your book, such as the writing process, your research, or the inspiration behind your story.

Create polls: Create polls to gather feedback from your followers, and use this feedback to make your book even better.

Host giveaways and contests: Host giveaways and contests on social media to engage with your audience and build excitement around your book.

In conclusion, social media can be a powerful tool for promoting your self-published ebook and reaching a wider audience. By following best practices, engaging with your audience, and using strategies such as sharing updates, offering promotions and incentives, and creating polls, you can increase your book's visibility and reach more potential readers.

Chapter V. Partnering with Influencers and Book Bloggers

The power of influencer marketing

How to find influencers and book bloggers in your niche

Best practices for working with influencers and book bloggers

Partnering with influencers and book bloggers can be a highly effective way to promote your self-published eBook and reach a wider audience. In this chapter, we'll discuss the power of influencer marketing, how to find influencers and book bloggers in your niche, and best practices for working with influencers and book bloggers.

The Power of Influencer Marketing

Reach a new audience: Influencer marketing allows you to reach a new audience and introduce your book to potential readers who may not have discovered it otherwise.

Increased credibility: When influencers and book bloggers recommend your book, it increases the credibility of your book and helps build trust with potential readers.

Cost-effective: Compared to other forms of advertising, influencer marketing can be a more cost-effective way to promote your book.

How to Find Influencers and Book Bloggers in Your Niche

Research: Start by researching influencers and book bloggers in your niche. Look for those who have a large following, a strong engagement rate, and a focus on your genre or theme.

Network: Attend literary events and conferences, and join online communities related to your niche to network with potential influencers and book bloggers.

Use tools: Use tools such as Buzzsumo and Google to search for influencers and book bloggers in your niche.

Best Practices for Working with Influencers and Book Bloggers

Build a relationship: Take the time to build a relationship with influencers and book bloggers. This means engaging with their content, commenting on their posts, and sharing their content on your own social media accounts.

Provide a copy of your book: Offer influencers and book bloggers a copy of your book for review. This allows them to get to know your work and potentially write a review or share their thoughts on their platform.

Be transparent: Be transparent in your partnerships with influencers and book bloggers. Clearly outline your expectations and goals, and be open and honest in your communication.

Offer incentives: Consider offering incentives to influencers and book bloggers for promoting your book, such as a commission on sales or exclusive content.

In conclusion, partnering with influencers and book bloggers can be a highly effective way to promote your self-published ebook and reach a wider audience. By building relationships, providing a copy of your book, and offering incentives, you can form valuable partnerships with influencers and book bloggers that will help you reach your goals and promote your book effectively.

Chapter VI. Giveaways and Contests

How to run a successful giveaway or contest

Best practices for running a giveaway or contest

Strategies for maximizing the impact of your giveaway or contest

Giveaways and contests can be an effective way to generate buzz and increase visibility for your self-published eBook. In this chapter, we'll discuss how to run a successful giveaway or contest, best practices for running a giveaway or contest, and strategies for maximizing the impact of your giveaway or contest.

How to Run a Successful Giveaway or Contest

Determine your goal: Before running a giveaway or contest, it's important to determine your goal. Are you looking to increase your social media following, generate reviews, or simply give back to your readers? Understanding your goal will help you determine the best type of giveaway or contest to run.

Choose the right platform: Choose a platform that is easy to use and provides the features you need to run your giveaway or contest. For example, if you're looking to increase your social media following, choose a platform that integrates with your social media accounts.

Set clear rules: Set clear rules for your giveaway or contest, including how to enter, how winners will be selected, and any restrictions or limitations.

Promote your giveaway or contest: Promote your giveaway or contest on your website, social media accounts, and email list. Consider partnering with influencers or book bloggers to reach a wider audience.

Best Practices for Running a Giveaway or Contest

Keep it simple: Keep your giveaway or contest simple and easy to understand. The more complicated the rules and requirements, the less likely people will be to participate.

Offer a valuable prize: Offer a prize that is valuable and relevant to your target audience. This can be a signed copy of your book, a gift card, or a related item.

Make it shareable: Encourage participants to share your giveaway or contest with their friends and followers. This will help you reach a wider audience and increase the impact of your giveaway or contest.

Strategies for Maximizing the Impact of Your Giveaway or Contest

Timing: Choose the right time to run your giveaway or contest. Consider running it during a holiday or other special event to generate more interest.

Collaborate: Consider collaborating with other authors or businesses in your niche to offer a larger prize or reach a wider audience.

Engage with participants: Engage with participants during and after your giveaway or contest. This will help build a relationship with your audience and increase the impact of your giveaway or contest.

In conclusion, giveaways and contests can be an effective way to generate buzz and increase visibility for your self-published eBook. By determining your goal, choosing the right platform, and offering a valuable prize, you can run a successful giveaway or contest that helps you reach your goals and promote your book effectively.

Chapter VII. Free Previews and Excerpts

The benefits of offering free previews and excerpts

How to create effective previews and excerpts

Strategies for using previews and excerpts to drive sales

Offering free previews and excerpts of your self-published eBook can be a powerful tool for promoting your book and driving sales. In this chapter, we'll discuss the benefits of offering free previews and excerpts, how to create effective previews and excerpts, and strategies for using previews and excerpts to drive sales.

The Benefits of Offering Free Previews and Excerpts

Increased visibility: Offering free previews and excerpts of your book can increase visibility and help you reach a wider audience.

Improved discoverability: Previews and excerpts can help potential readers discover your book and learn more about your writing style.

Increased credibility: By offering free previews and excerpts, you can demonstrate your confidence in your work and build credibility with potential readers.

Increased sales: By offering a taste of your book, you can entice potential readers to purchase the full version.

How to Create Effective Previews and Excerpts

Choose the right length: Choose a length that is long enough to give potential readers a good sense of your writing style and the content of your book, but short enough to keep them interested and engaged.

Highlight your strengths: Choose passages that showcase your writing style, the quality of your research, or other strengths of your book.

Make it shareable: Make your previews and excerpts shareable, either by offering them as a standalone document or embedding them on your website or social media accounts.

Strategies for Using Previews and Excerpts to Drive Sales

Offer them for free: Offer your previews and excerpts for free on your website or through a distribution platform. This can help you reach a wider audience and increase visibility for your book.

Use them to build your email list: Offer your previews and excerpts as an incentive for people to join your email list. This can help you build a relationship with your audience and promote your book effectively.

Promote them on social media: Promote your previews and excerpts on your social media accounts and encourage your followers to share them with their friends and followers.

Offer them as a bonus: Offer your previews and excerpts as a bonus for people who purchase your book. This can encourage people to purchase the full version and increase sales.

In conclusion, offering free previews and excerpts of your self-published ebook can be a powerful tool for promoting your book and driving sales. By choosing the right length, highlighting your strengths, and making them shareable, you can create effective previews and excerpts that help you reach your goals and promote your book effectively.

Chapter VIII. Offering Free Bonus Content

The benefits of offering free bonus content

How to create effective bonus content

Strategies for using bonus content to drive sales

Offering free bonus content can be an effective way to promote your self-published ebook and drive sales. In this chapter, we'll discuss the benefits of offering free bonus content, how to create effective bonus content, and strategies for using bonus content to drive sales.

The Benefits of Offering Free Bonus Content

Increased value: Offering free bonus content can increase the perceived value of your book and make it more appealing to potential readers.

Improved engagement: Bonus content can encourage readers to engage with your book and explore it in more depth.

Increased sales: By offering free bonus content, you can entice potential readers to purchase your book and increase sales.

Improved customer satisfaction: By offering free bonus content, you can improve customer satisfaction and build loyalty among your audience.

How to Create Effective Bonus Content

Choose the right type of content: Choose bonus content that complements your book and adds value for your audience. This can include behind-the-scenes information, additional research, or additional chapters.

Make it relevant: Make sure your bonus content is relevant to your book and your audience. This will help you keep your audience engaged and interested in your work.

Make it shareable: Make your bonus content shareable, either by offering it as a standalone document or embedding it on your website or social media accounts.

Strategies for Using Bonus Content to Drive Sales

Offer it as an incentive: Offer your bonus content as an incentive for people to purchase your book. This can encourage people to buy your book and increase sales.

Promote it on social media: Promote your bonus content on your social media accounts and encourage your followers to share it with their friends and followers.

Use it to build your email list: Offer your bonus content as an incentive for people to join your email list. This can help you build a relationship with your audience and promote your book effectively.

Offer it as a bonus for positive reviews: Offer your bonus content as a bonus for people who leave positive reviews for your book. This can encourage people to leave positive reviews and promote your book effectively.

In conclusion, offering free bonus content can be an effective way to promote your self-published eBook and drive sales. By choosing the right type of content, making it relevant and shareable, and using it effectively, you can create bonus content that helps you reach your goals and promote your book effectively.

Chapter IX. Build a Literary Empire from Home

Start a few side hustles and establish your writing career

As more of us work from home it is now possible to do most of our work remotely. Being a writer, it is possible to create an article, an eBook, a report, a presentation and publish it online in a short period of time.

Your desk at home is now the main operating centre for almost all your literary endeavours. You can create a podcast, attend a Zoom meeting online with other writers or your readers, do a bit of blogging about your favourite topics, manage your social media platforms and complete a writing project, all while sitting at your desk at home.

Building your literary empire from home is a real possibility. You can start small and then gradually increase your efforts to increase your income and your authority as a professional writer. Start with a few side hustles for now and then grow them over time.

Plan: Create a strategy and a plan to develop a profitable writing career. Write all the features of the plan, leaving no stone unturned and no opportunity lost.

Books: Start writing your first book, fiction or non-fiction. Publish your book on Amazon KDP, Draft2Digital, Smashwords, or on any other print-on-demand publishing platform. It is never too late to start writing, if you like writing short stories, write a couple and publish them by the weekend. Once published, blog about it, talk about it on social media, from Twitter to YouTube and Instagram.

Paid Articles: Write articles for money and publish them weekly or daily, the choice is yours. First, do research online to find those websites that pay for articles. Pick a few popular niches and start writing on them.

Advertising & Copywriting: Do a course in advertising and copywriting, so that you are familiar with the skills of copywriting and advertising. After you have completed the course successfully, go on to set up your own independent copywriting enterprise. I did a course in Copywriting from AWAI (American Writers and Artists Institute) and it was worth it. It helps to learn how to do advertising so that you can do your own promotional campaigns.

Social Media Management: Do a short diploma course in social media management or do a free course. You will definitely benefit from knowing all that is essential in your freelancing as a Social Media Manager. It does help if you set up your own social media accounts from Twitter to Instagram and TikTok. Start as soon as possible, so that you can gain followers who will follow your posts. Your followers today are future customers tomorrow.

Courses: Using your literary skills set up your own short and long courses on any subjects that you are interested in teaching. You can convert your books into modules for a short course. Create a number of instruction videos for the course. Prepare assignments for each module of the course. Next, you need to select a great course publishing platform. Do a bit of research and you will find a few course platforms looking for entrepreneurs to set up their courses.

Audio Books: Convert your books into audiobooks, either by hiring someone to read your books or by doing the narration yourself. There are a few websites that have professionals who can read your books for audio recordings.

Revenue Share: Join a revenue share website like Medium, where you get a portion of the income from the number of readers who read your writings.

Public Speaking: As a writer, published author, advertiser, course creator, you will definitely be in demand as a public speaker. Do a little publicity informing organizations in your field of interest that you are open to giving speeches about your work or on any topic in your field.

Email: There are companies that require freelancers to respond to emails. Look for these jobs on the web to earn an additional income.

Editing and Proofreading: Advertise your editing and proofreading services. As a writer, we are all familiar with the editing and proofreading we need to do before sending out anything to publish.

Podcasting: Create your own podcast and tell the world about your life, your work, and how you do what you do best, which is writing and publishing.

Hourly Consulting: Take on the role of a writing and publishing consultant or as a writing coach, you can charge by the hour for your services.

Investing: Do not waste your literary income, treat all income like you would from a regular job and invest it well. Profits invested today will help you through many a rainy day.

Fundraising: Take on the role of a Fundraiser, creating promotional materials for organizations that employ you for your advertising and publicity services.

Templates: Create personalized templates for blogs, websites, banners, and social media platforms for firms that employ you.

Blogging: Maintain at least two blogs to advertise and promote your writing and freelancing career. Monetize your blogs with advertising, keep them updated and your visitors informed with the help of a newsletter.

Private Facebook Groups: Make your own private Facebook group or one for a client where people are charged to join the group.

Niche and Authority websites: Make a niche website on a particular topic for yourself or your clients. Develop an authority website on a subject, containing whatever there is to know about it. Once the website is established as an authority or trusted website, you will not be short on clients lining up to gain the benefits of your expertise.

Special Reports: Compile and create special reports for your clients. Keeping all the elements which are needed by your customer, develop and present an impressive special report for them and they will be coming back for more business.

It is important to bear in mind that just as "Rome was not built in a day", you need to persist in your writing work. Keep building your income-generating streams and before long, they will automatically create monthly income for you. This is not easily done, but it docs help to adapt to the wants and needs of readers and customers, as well as the changing world we are living in today.

Chapter X. Making Your Writer's Brand and Logo

Selling Your Talent and Skills Successfully as a Writer

I have always loved the Shield in Heraldic designs. This is a direct influence from my father who studied Heraldry, Logos, and Monogram designs.

You can make your own Logo and start creating your writer brand today on Canva[1]. There are so many wonderful designs and you will find it very interesting to prepare your own logo.

All the designs on this page were created by me on Canva. You could also visit Fiverr to get a freelance designer to prepare your Writer's Branding portfolio.

When I went about setting up my Author Brand these are a few steps I took:

1. **Website**: Creating my website, where my brand is advertised for the world to see. The website is a portfolio of my work.

2. **Blog**: I have my own blog, which is most important, and which I have for over two decades now.

3. **social media**: I have my social media accounts on Twitter, Facebook, and Instagram, which help me to send out my literary news to my followers.

4. **Theme**: A positive message is the theme of all my writings, whether it is fiction, poetry, or non-fiction.

---

1. https://www.canva.com/

5. **Potential:** I like to try out different writing styles and create different literary presentations with my work. I attempt to maximize my potential as a writer.

6. **Expression**: My work is an expression of my mind and my creativity. I like to push the boundaries of my imagination, through my fiction and in my articles.

7. **Aim, Objective, and Life Purpose**: The primary aim and objective of my writing are to make the world a more positive place. My life purpose is to help people to enjoy reading my work and to help me grow and develop as a writer.

8. **Opportunities:** I am always on the lookout for more unique ideas to put into my writings. I look forward to trying out new publishing platforms so that my work can reach a wider and diverse audience. I am happy to have re-discovered Medium after about seven years since I first joined.

9. **Self-Knowledge**: My writing is a journey in self-discovery, as it gives me an opportunity to discover who I am as a person.

10. **Author Brand**: Every piece of writing done by me is a reflection of my identity, my creativity, and my Author Brand. I am enthusiastic about my literary, artistic work and it is my personal brand sealed with my signature of creativity.

When creating your Author Brand always keep in mind three vital elements:

A. You must believe in yourself, your identity, and your life purpose as an author. You can do your best work by looking into your life and identity. You are your best resource for stories and ideas. *One day you will be able to say, that you have established your Author Identity with your Author Brand!*

Warren Comics was my Brand when I published my first graphic novel, "Pandemic Blasters"[1], as an e-book and as a paperback.

B. You should go out to find all the opportunities to help you to live to your true potential as an Author. Every idea, innovation, and development in the field of writing and publishing is an opportunity for you to maximize your potential as an Author.

C. Your Author Brand keeps developing and transforming over time, the same way you keep maturing as an author in your craft. The logo above is the one that I use on Substack[2]. On Substack, this is my Brand Image, which states that I am a creative and imaginative writer with interesting literary work.

Writing is a learning experience, have fun, enjoy yourself, become famous, make money creating your literary work because there is no one who best represents your Brand, but YOU!

---

1. https://books2read.com/pandemic

2. https://warrenbrown.substack.com/

Chapter XI. Lone Ranger of Entrepreneurship

If you have been an entrepreneur for some time, you know that it is for most of the time, up to you to create, manage and promote your brand. There could be months when you have not done enough product creation of promotion and the result will be that your brand suffers in the marketplace. Do you feel that you are a Lone Ranger in the field of Entrepreneurship?

Entrepreneurship requires dedication and hard work and sometimes quite a bit of effort on your part and it can financially cost a large sum of money to have your product or service put in front of your target market. An entrepreneur can advertise on sites like Google and Yahoo and get a substantial amount of traffic to visit his or her site.

A well-designed opt-in page is required for any website. *An opt-in page is of extreme importance as it collects email addresses for the website owner.* The email addresses represent prospective customers who would be interested in the product or the service which is advertised on the website. However, people do not give their emails for nothing in return. It is always good to offer a free product or service which your website visitors would need. Website visitors will gladly enter their email address for a free PDF Report or for a Discount code, which looks attractive to them.

Advertising is very important for any website. A person can build an elaborate and well-designed site, but the only problem could be that there is low or no site traffic or visitors to the site. *It is essential for the advertiser to select the best advertising platform, the right niche and target market in order to get "buying traffic".* Visitors who are willing to spend money is referred to as "buying traffic".

Product creation or choosing the right type of service to offer is also an important feature in Entrepreneurship. An entrepreneur needs to do sufficient research into his or her Niche (area of interest) and target market, with the help of keywords to know where a demand and market exists for what he or she has to offer in the Marketplace.

A Lone Ranger Entrepreneur will not survive in an e-economy or in any marketplace. Even the Lone Ranger has his trusted friend Tonto to assist him in all his adventures in the Wild West.

An entrepreneur needs a network of friends, customers and members to support him in his or her ventures. I would like to suggest that you should also join an entrepreneur platform, which can help you to build a network of friends and Associates, who would be like your own trusted friend Tonto. *Build your online presence and brand today.*

"Hi-Yo Silver! Away!" says the Lone Ranger, as he rides off towards the sunrise of Entrepreneurship, accompanied by his trusted friend Tonto.

Chapter XII. The Golden Rule for Postcard Marketing your Books

Every writer needs to have a few of these "magnetic" postcards

Postcards published by writers are great for marketing purposes. We all feel that postcards are old-fashioned. With Postcard Marketing it has been noted that 51% of postcards are read and 20% of readers are likely to respond.

Postcards are effective tools for the following reasons:

- Generate sales leads for your latest book launch.
- Introduce a new eBook, book or course to a new audience.
- Get feedback from your readers.
- Promote special offers on your back catalogue of materials.
- Keep in touch with existing readers, followers and writers.
- Drive traffic to your latest book release.

Always Remember the Golden Rule in all your Marketing efforts both online and offline:

Success depends on making the right offer to the right people in the right way at the right time.

Every Writer needs to include postcards in their marketing campaigns. The festive season is around the corner and authors are now gearing up with producing and marketing their latest content online and offline.

Postcards are like magnets for your readers and more authors need to produce them to promote their work. I love collecting bookmarks and postcards just because they are colorful and the graphics look great.

Chapter XIII. The Juggernaut Writer

The Ultimate Dream for almost every writer today

A goal I would love to achieve someday, like the prolific writers of the past and present.

I have done it again and coined a new term, the "Juggernaut Writer." A "Juggernaut" by definition is "a huge, powerful and overwhelming force." Therefore, a "Juggernaut Writer" would be an individual who has the ability and the capacity to produce a large body of material regularly. A prolific writer on literary steroids (not literally) would be a "Juggernaut Writer".

What could a "Juggernaut Writer" produce and how would he or she go about training to become one such writer?

Here are a few essential points to train and to become the "Ultimate Juggernaut Writer."

1. Write daily, from one article a day to a maximum of five to ten articles.
2. Develop an interest in a large number of topics, themes, and issues.
3. Write poems, stories, articles, blog posts, stories, novels, try your hand at everything.
4. Always look for novel ways and methods to express your literary creativity.
5. Publish your work on many publishing platforms.
6. Encourage others to write as well as get inspired by other prolific writers.
7. Keep several journals on a variety of topics, so that you always have a large body of materials to use.
8. Stories are present everywhere; it is up to you as a Juggernaut

writer to use everything you observe to create posts.

9. Add your unique perspective to everything that you write. In this way, you create your own literary signature and style.

10. Read the feedback from your followers and readers. Use that feedback to draw inspiration from and to gear you towards writing more interesting materials with passion and enthusiasm.

I have always loved challenging myself and then giving myself a pat on the back for having accomplished every personal challenge I set myself. It makes life more interesting and gives me a sense of accomplishment. I know that I can do whatever I put my mind to if I try.

These personal literary challenges help me as a writer to increase my love and enthusiasm for expressing my creativity and imagination through my writings.

On the 30th of January 2021, I completed my 1-day Medium Writing Challenge. I wanted to see how many articles I could write in a day. This was a personal challenge. I had set myself just for the thrill and the excitement.

Chapter XIV. The Pizza Slice Writing Method

Dividing a story into tasty portions for your readers to enjoy

I use the *Pizza Slice Writing Method* when I write and publish my work online. I have given this method a name. Curiouser and curiouser this gets, so what is the Pizza Slice Writing Method?

A pizza is a delicious preparation of Italian origin consisting of a flat round base made out of dough which is baked with a topping of cheese, tomatoes and other fish, meat, vegetables, anchovies, onions, mushrooms, olives and pineapples. Once the pizza is baked all you need to do is slice it into portions and enjoy a delicious meal, one slice at a time. Every slice taste as delicious as the one before. This is because every slice is filled with all the same delectable components. Even though it is just a slice, it has all the properties of the whole pizza.

Here are a few of the key features of PSWM when writing:

1. Write a long story, poem, or article and pack it with a lot of interesting facts and other nuggets of useful information.
2. Publish the long story, poem or article, as soon as possible.
3. After the work has been completed, dissect the whole piece into smaller sections. Each section must contain an interesting fact.
4. Develop each dissected section of the long article into smaller articles.
5. Publish your smaller articles as soon as they are finished.
6. You will notice that each part can be developed into a full-blown piece of work.
7. This practice of dividing an article into smaller portions, will help you to brainstorm, as new ideas begin to start flowing.
8. With the PSWM you will notice that not only will your output increase, but you will be writing more creative materials every

time.

9. This exercise will also help your mind to become more imaginative and creative. Once started you will find that it is so much easier to keep writing on a regular basis.

10. The PSWM will result in you getting noticed as a prolific writer. You will eventually become an authority on the subject or subjects you write and publish.

Chapter XV. Conclusion

A summary of the key takeaways from the eBook

Final thoughts and advice for maximizing sales through free eBook distribution.

In this eBook, we have explored the various methods and avenues to distribute your self-published eBook for free in order to maximize sales. From choosing the right platform to utilizing social media, partnering with influencers and book bloggers, running giveaways and contests, offering free previews and excerpts, and providing free bonus content, there are many ways to promote your eBook and drive sales.

Key Takeaways:

Choose the right platform for your book: Consider features such as ease of use, accessibility, and distribution reach when choosing an eBook distribution platform.

Utilize social media: social media can be an effective way to promote your book and engage with your audience. Consider strategies such as posting regular updates, engaging with followers, and partnering with influencers.

Partner with influencers and book bloggers: Influencer marketing can be an effective way to promote your book and reach a wider audience. Make sure to find influencers and book bloggers who are a good fit for your book and niche.

Run giveaways and contests: Giveaways and contests can be an effective way to promote your book and drive sales. Make sure to run them effectively and follow best practices.

Offer free previews and excerpts: Offer free previews and excerpts of your book to entice potential readers to purchase the full book.

Provide free bonus content: Offer free bonus content as an incentive for people to purchase your book and improve customer satisfaction.

Final Thoughts and Advice:

Be consistent: Consistency is key when it comes to promoting your book and driving sales. Make sure to post regular updates and engage with your audience on a regular basis.

Be creative: Get creative when promoting your book and trying new things to see what works best for you and your audience.

Stay focused: Stay focused on your goals and what you want to achieve with your book. This will help you stay motivated and on track.

In conclusion, promoting your self-published eBook for free can be an effective way to maximize sales and reach a wider audience. By following the best practices and strategies outlined in this eBook, you can effectively promote your book and achieve your goals.

Don't miss out!

Visit the website below and you can sign up to receive emails whenever Warren Brown publishes a new book. There's no charge and no obligation.

https://books2read.com/r/B-A-LFGF-MCMFC

BOOKS 2 READ

Connecting independent readers to independent writers.

Did you love *Quick Guide to Increasing Sales for Your Magnetic E-Book*?
Then you should read *Rewrite Your Story To Become The Hero*[1] by
Warren Brown!

You are the only person who can live your story.

Do you feel that you are the Hero of your story?

You can rewrite the story of your life, re-invent your life and become the Hero of your story.

You can attract everything you want with the power of your mind. Your mind is a powerful magnet that needs to be switched on for you to attract all that you need in life. You have been attracting everything in your life till this very instant. Your mind has brought you to read this book, because it is what you need to guide you on your path to fulfilling your destiny.

---

1. https://books2read.com/u/31rv77

2. https://books2read.com/u/31rv77

Using the Power of Auto-suggestion you can attract all that you want in life. Change your destiny and become the Hero you were meant to become in life.

Read more at https://warren4.wixsite.com/warren.

Also by Warren Brown

Prolific Writing for Everyone
On Writing Magic
The Writer's Creativity Cave
The Writer's Oasis
Castle of Ideas and Inspiration for Writers
Chasm of Creativity and Inspiration For Writers

Standalone
Supernova: A Collection of Science Fiction Short Stories
Instant Poetry App
Mask of Evil: Adventures of the Storyteller
Vintage Tales: Eurasian Short Stories
Impostor Assassin
Camelot Crypto 1- Crypto Genesis
Camelot Crypto 2- Crypto Odyssey
Camelot Crypto 3- Crypto Symbiosis
Camelot Crypto: Three Short Crypto-currency Stories
Three Christmas Coins: A Poem
The Christmas Dimension
Happy New Year
Festive Delights
Coulrophobia: Empire of the Clown King

Creative Vibes
Rewrite Your Story To Become The Hero
Pandemic Blasters
New Year Odyssey
Pandemic Blasters Omnibus
Travel Man
Monkey in Mind
Masquerade
The Marauders and Mavericks
Mystic Inspiration Prompts for Writers
Cafe of Creativity and Inspiration For Writers
Quick Guide to Increasing Sales for Your Magnetic E-Book

Watch for more at https://warren4.wixsite.com/warren.

About the Author

Warren Brown is an Author who has written in several genres from fiction to non-fiction. Warren is a certified Life Coach and Hypnotherapist. Warren completed his Advertising and Copywriting training through American Writers and Artists Inc. (AWAI). I have been an Indie publisher for over eleven years now. I have been writing and publishing on the web since 1993. Website:

https://warren4.wixsite.com/warren

Medium:

https://warrenauthor.medium.com/

Substack:

https://warrenbrown.substack.com/

Read more at https://warren4.wixsite.com/warren.

www.ingramcontent.com/pod-product-compliance
Lightning Source LLC
Chambersburg PA
CBHW060500160726
47992CB00003B/1255